To the givers who continue to inspire me.

Thank you to Dorothy Vogel; and to Emily Ann Francisco, curatorial assistant,
and Molly Donovan, curator of art, of the National Gallery of Art,
for their continued support and encouragement.
—J.A.K.

For those who embrace change!
—J.B.

Text copyright © 2021 Jackie Azúa Kramer
Illustrations copyright © 2021 Julia Breckenreid

Book design by Melissa Nelson Greenberg

Pages 8 (white bunny) and 21 (red bunny) © 2021 Ray Johnson Estate /
Artists Rights Society (ARS), New York

Page 21 (Warhol figure) © 2021 The Andy Warhol Foundation for the Visual Arts, Inc. /
Licensed by Artists Rights Society (ARS), New York

Library of Congress Cataloging-in-Publication Data available.
ISBN: 978-1-951836-21-4

Printed in China • 10 9 8 7 6 5 4 3 2 1

CAMERON KIDS is an imprint of CAMERON + COMPANY

CAMERON + COMPANY
Petaluma, California
www.cameronbooks.com

DOROTHY & HERBERT

An Ordinary Couple and Their Extraordinary Collection of Art

Jackie Azúa Kramer • Julia Breckenreid

cameron kids

Dorothy and Herbert lived for **ART**.

At a noisy New York City post office,
Herbert hand-sorted the last of the mail.
He grabbed his drawing pad
and dashed to catch a subway
DOWNTOWN.

At the quiet Brooklyn Public Library, Dorothy put away large reference books. She checked her bag for her sketchbook and hurried to catch a subway **UPTOWN**.

Dorothy and Herbert Vogel
didn't want to be late for their painting class.

Inspired by abstract expressionism,
they loved the freedom of the brushstrokes,
the looseness of the lines, and the playful patterns.

As a newly married couple,
they honeymooned at the National Gallery of Art,
spending days gazing at masterpieces.

In New York City, in the 1960s,
artists' studios had begun to pop up
in the SoHo neighborhood,
crowded with street and performance art.

And when there was a new museum exhibit
or gallery show in town,
Dorothy and Herbert were always there,
hand in hand.

Art filled them with **WONDER**.

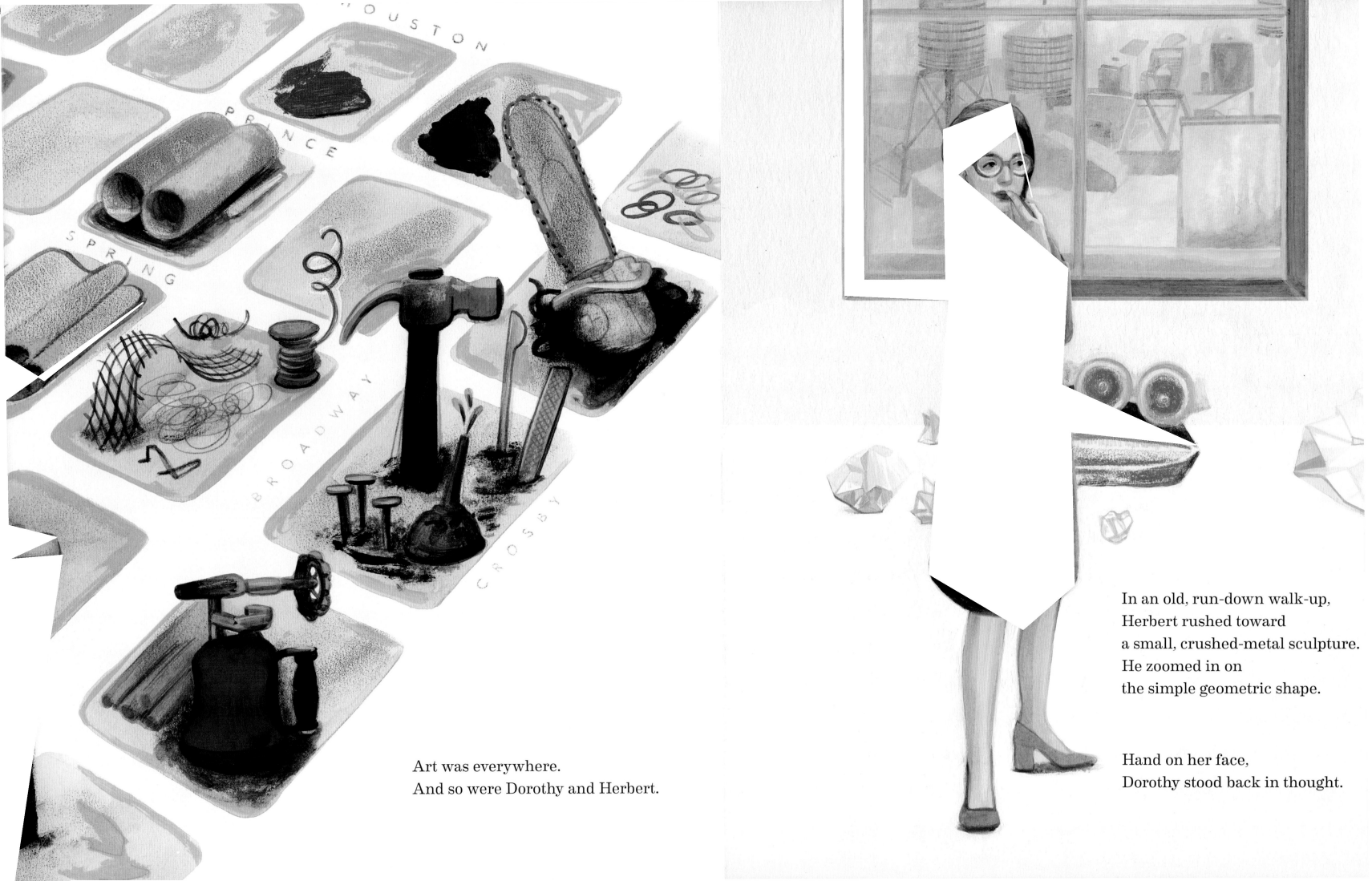

Art was everywhere.
And so were Dorothy and Herbert.

In an old, run-down walk-up,
Herbert rushed toward
a small, crushed-metal sculpture.
He zoomed in on
the simple geometric shape.

Hand on her face,
Dorothy stood back in thought.

The use of everyday materials
like rusted car metal was unusual.
And the primary colors
were surprising and fun.

WE'LL TAKE IT!

Inspired by their first art purchase,
Dorothy and Herbert wanted to see everything.

Listen and talk to the **ARTISTS**.

Share and discuss **IDEAS**.

They became trusted mentors
in their artistic process.

Dorothy and Herbert loved
the work of these new artists
so much, they stopped painting.

And on a penny-wise and thrifty budget,
they not only collected art,
they became **ART COLLECTORS**.

If Dorothy and Herbert liked the art,
could carry it in a cab or subway . . .

move it up the elevator,
and fit it into
their tiny Upper East Side apartment,
they bought it.

They even traded cat-sitting for a
collage from an artist couple.

Herbert and Dorothy's curious cats,
Manet, Renoir, and Archie,
watched rooms burst with art,
modular cubes,
a rubber rug.

The turtles and fish gazed from their aquarium
at ink drawings and paper sculptures.

The bathroom walls
swayed and shimmied in red dots
and yellow squiggles.

Even under their bed—
boxes of art and dust bunnies.

Dorothy and Herbert's mini museum inspired **CREATIVITY**.

Artists made new works on the spot.

And in their small kitchen,
Dorothy and Herbert shared their favorite
scallion pancakes and fortune cookies.

Word got out to the art world
of the librarian and the postal clerk's
EXTRAORDINARY collection.

And soon Dorothy and Herbert planned
for their own gallery debut.

Dorothy and Herbert were all the **BUZZ**.

After many years, Dorothy and Herbert's collection reflected their love of art, and now they wanted to share it with the world.

They chose the National Gallery of Art,
a museum they had always loved
and where everyone can see the art for free.

On moving day, Dorothy and Herbert watched as,
piece by piece, their priceless collection moved out.

From such a small space came so much.
And it kept coming, and coming . . .
Thousands of artworks filled four huge moving vans.

Not long after the movers were gone,
Dorothy and Herbert stood in
their empty apartment,
A BLANK CANVAS.

On a bare wall
they hung something new.

Something that filled them with wonder again.

MOST OF US GO THROUGH THE WORLD NEVER SEEING ANYTHING. THEN YOU MEET SOMEBODY LIKE HERB AND DOROTHY WHO HAVE EYES THAT SEE.
—RICHARD TUTTLE, ARTIST

AUTHOR'S NOTE

When my daughter was just four years old, I took her on her first big city adventure to the Museum of Modern Art in NYC. I love art! As a writer, art is one of my greatest sources of inspiration. So it was destined for me to discover the storied life of Dorothy and Herbert Vogel in an amazing documentary. As I watched, I became transfixed by their love and dedication to visual artists, their process and final works. I had the pleasure of exchanging correspondence with Dorothy. What she shared, simply, is her continued passion for the many, many works of art she and Herbert gave away for the world to see.

Herbert, a postal clerk in New York City, and Dorothy, a librarian at the Brooklyn Public Library, didn't have a formal education in art. They felt enjoying art is about discovering things that you find fun to look at. Their favorite was minimalist and conceptual art.

Beginning in the 1960s, they bought and collected thousands of sculptures, paintings, mobiles, and drawings from such luminaries as Sol LeWitt, Chuck Close, and Christo and Jeanne-Claude. The art was placed everywhere in their one-bedroom Manhattan apartment, including the kitchen, bathroom, inside closets, under the bed, and even on the ceiling!

In addition to art, Herbert and Dorothy loved animals. Wandering around the collection were their many cats, named for famous artists like Manet and Renoir. They also had large turtles and fish in an aquarium who gazed through glass at their fascinating and growing collection.

Dorothy (1935–) and Herbert (1922–2012) remind us that anyone can understand, love, and collect art. In 1992, the Vogels gave their priceless collection, over two thousand works, to the National Gallery of Art in Washington, D.C. And then they started collecting and filling up their empty apartment with thousands of works of art all over again. In 2008, they created the *Dorothy and Herbert Vogel Collection: Fifty Works for Fifty States*, gifting an additional fifty works of art to public museums in fifty states! Dorothy and Herbert continued to collect and give art to the National Gallery until Herbert's death in 2012. And Dorothy continues to give.

ILLUSTRATOR'S NOTE

I am delighted to have had the opportunity to visually tell the story of the Vogels. These extraordinary people were passionate about supporting artists, so curious and joyful in their pursuit of understanding new ideas. This, coupled with their generosity, is so important for kids (big and small) to know about. Fostering curiosity about the world and being open to different people's perspectives is imperative.

I had a lot of fun and learned a lot while researching and planning out my drawings for this book. I went down many rabbit holes, searching for ways to show you the art of that time, in order to give you little clues and conceptual twists of my own to each illustration in the book. Showing you how I think through the images I create is so important to me—I like to think of it as a puzzle for you to solve—and it's my way of telling a story! My hope is that when you read this book, you'll see something new each time. If you're wondering about who some of the artists are in the illustrations, please have a look at my website (www.breckenreid.com) for their names and where you can find their works.

JACKIE HAS CAPTURED THE SPIRIT OF OUR LIFE WITH ART. THE TRUTH IS THAT I DIDN'T KNOW ANYTHING ABOUT ART WHEN I MET HERB. I LEARNED FROM HIM. WHEN WE MARRIED, HE WAS INTERESTED IN PAINTING AND SO I TOOK COURSES IN PAINTING, TOO. I WANTED TO BE AN ARTIST LIKE HIM. WE HUNG OUR OWN WORKS ON OUR WALLS. THEN WE BEGAN TO COLLECT ART AND STARTED TO REPLACE OUR WORKS WITH ONES WE BOUGHT. AFTER A FEW YEARS, WE DECIDED WE WERE BETTER AT COLLECTING THAN PAINTING, SO WE GAVE IT UP.

ART CAN BE FUN TO ENJOY, TO COLLECT, AND TO LIVE WITH, FOR PEOPLE OF ALL AGES. YOU DON'T NEED LOTS OF KNOWLEDGE OF ART TO LOOK AT AND LIKE A PAINTING OR A SCULPTURE. JUST LIKE YOU DON'T NEED INFORMATION TO PET A CAT. WHAT YOU NEED IS AN OPEN MIND. YOU CAN EVEN MAKE YOUR OWN ART. HAVE FUN.

—LOVE, DOROTHY

Dorothy and Herbert Vogel, 1975

Photograph © The Estate of Nathaniel Tileston

To view the Vogels' collection of art, visit the National Gallery of Art, Washington, D.C., in person or online at www.nga.gov. For additional museums in your state, and to view the Vogels' entire collection, visit vogel5050.org.

ABSTRACT EXPRESSIONISM: The leading artistic movement in the 1940s and 1950s, abstract expressionism was the first to place New York City at the forefront of international modern art. The movement is characterized by bold, gestural abstraction in all mediums, particularly large painted canvases.

AVANT-GARDE: As applied to art, avant-garde means art that is innovative, introducing or exploring new forms or subject matter.

CONCEPTUAL ART: This style of art emerged in the late 1960s, emphasizing ideas rather than the creation of visual forms. Conceptual artists used their work to question what art is.

MINIMALISM: This mostly American artistic movement of the 1960s focuses on simplicity in basic geometric shapes and primary colors.

MODULAR: This is a term used particularly in relation to minimalism, referring to a work of art with constituent parts that can be moved, separated, and recombined.

Examples of abstract, avant-garde, conceptual, and minimalist artists include Sol LeWitt, Richard Tuttle, Robert Mangold, Chuck Close, Roy Lichtenstein, Lucio Pozzi, Pat Steir, Lynda Benglis, James Siena, Jeff Koons, Christo and Jeanne-Claude, and Cindy Sherman.

SOURCES:

Paul Gardner, "An Extraordinary Gift of Art from Ordinary People," *Smithsonian* magazine, October 1992.

John T. Paoletti and Ruth Fine; *From Minimal to Conceptual Art: Works from the Dorothy and Herbert Vogel Collection*; Washington, D.C.; National Gallery of Art; 1994.

Megumi Sasaki, director; *Herb and Dorothy*; Arthouse Films; Fine Line Media Inc.; 2008.

National Gallery of Art: www.nga.gov

Vogel 50x50: vogel5050.org